AMANTE

SYLVIA PLANT

To Pranav, in whose eyes I am a good egg.

Contents

Preface

I don't want us to be not included. I just want to be included. I want us to be partners.

Mrs. Barry, Anne With An E

1. Sisyphus in the making

I go to my mess,
the ones with chairs and tables.
I see fish aplenty,
and occasionally,
a seahorse and a few shrimps.
Lately, I have given up having fish of my own.
An aquarium with corals,
handpicked stones and
a moss-filled branch.
A box filled with *rasas*.
What if my box shatters?
What if the fishes try to seek freedom?
I will have another burden to carry.
I know.
The shrimps are less.
And so are the seahorses.
But what if there is a battle?

2. De Anima

I want a sea-facing room for possession
and a handy screen of my interest.
I may not use the sea but
I like how it sounds.
At brunch, I want a *dalgona* for my socials
and cutlery, minimalistic.
I may not touch the coffee but
I like how it looks.
I want a wild weed for peer-pressure
and *Nietzsche* to soothe my soul.
I may not like the strain but
I like how it smells.
In the evening, I want an old-fashioned for class
and carefully wrapped bacon.
I may not like the company but
I like how it feels.
I want a possessive character for a man
And a relationship, dominating.
I may not embrace the fear but
I like how it tastes.

3. Bosom Friend

If I have breasts,
I will have to protect them.
Not because they ache or
someone's inspecting.
Or because they are displaced.
It will simply restore my dignity
and uphold my right to be a woman
in this society of confusion.
It will help my desire to
trim them, and I will take a lot of pride
in this loan
for nothing so close to the heart
has ever been in vain.
In return, I will ask for a sew
and a needle
to help my skin
for I know that I'd be happy within.
You see, had I been a man
I would have brushed across the crowd
and reached the shore.
And no, I'm not refusing to walk the coast.
All I'm saying is
I have to cover my bosom
like a child hugs its mother
and it takes a lifetime

for someone
who does not have
a mother.
But what if for once
I let them free
and they tickle and tackle
around the block
surrounding the trees.
Will I have to cover their eyes
with my hands?
Or will the words leave me be?

You see, if I have breasts
I will have to shelter them
which I have to do
if I am a woman.

4. April is the cruellest month.

Why do you nurture that fibre back to black?
Why can't you let go
Of mummification?
After all, it may not be as useful
To your dead lover.
In a world full of ironies,
it may make little sense.
April is the cruellest month.
But what good does it do you
to add to the sweat?
Beauty is no excuse for
deliberate reincarnation.
What animality do you hide
beneath those locks
that you are ashamed to let it breathe?

5. Prostitute

I have appeared stronger
And my bones are made of diamonds,
For anyone who does not believe in themselves.
Explore me.
I have soothed a few hearts
Attended to an ailing marriage,
Severed my purity
And met another man who I helped birth anew
But I am the one who is
marginalised.
I have wailed, and I have arrived
At a better pedestal now
For I have eaten my guilt,
Before my guilt could smoulder me
Like a learned witch burning on the stake.

I have appeared stronger
And my bones are made of diamonds,
For anyone who does not believe in themselves.
Exploit me.
Whilst I met woman after woman
Who wrote poems, complimentary-shallow
On sex-trade
Not knowing, at the least
What it takes

To get up every morning and eat guilt
Like you were eating grains of barley.

I have appeared stronger
And my bones are made of diamonds,
For anyone who does not believe in themselves.
I exploded.
Whilst I met some men and many lovers
Who believed and preached that one could
Only accept it
When it was legalised.
"Is it a sign of manliness
If you willingly put your daughters
On the pedestal? ", they maintained.

6. Poetry

There's poetry in my naked skin.
There's poetry in each of my sins.
If you can't find it,
I'll urge you to look above your chin.

7. New Year

See me from another eye
but do not tell me if I'm mistaken or ambitious.
Tell me how I react and what I regret.
Show me a better way to validate myself;
feel my agonies and tell me otherwise.
Don't call Freud on me, I insist.
Don't make me go on a tirade
of I am and who I am not
or if I even
use words to describe my reactions,
Do not tell me to paint them with colours or
glorify my esteemed self to people as me.
Hold not the cup of my thoughts still
but spill it with your bare hands
and measure the loss in a bottle of absinthe
so I can be half-adorned.
Be my journal;
write me a letter of appreciation
for I have been a better human than before.
I have scaled the nearest mountain of mourning,
drank from the streams of sorrowful drowning,
and used my wisdom to build a tower of integrity.
Take me to a universe where hope questions hope
Use my biased observation of myself
and turn it against me.

Paint me through your eyes
and claim that art is never true.
Tell me you're not giving up on me.

• 10 •

8. Amante

What is nectar to a bee
or light to a leaf?
What is warmth to a child
or pea to a worm?
You are that to me.

9. This or that

My lines are often blurred
between what is right
and meddling in many affairs.
It is understandable.
To be left with the debris
is a bitter realisation and
mending things could be harsh.

10. Lucky Charm

Forgive me, for I am only examining my stakes here.
I don't mean to interrupt, but
you have a charm
greater than any lake I've surpassed
and kinder than a baby recently born.
Your words will linger around like
a vetiver in a closed closet.
And I shall not open it for hundred years
lest the smell comes off.
Forgive me, I am afraid.
It is usual.

www.ingramcontent.com/pod-product-compliance
Lightning Source LLC
Chambersburg PA
CBHW030512170726
47990CB00008BA/3165